ARTHUR MILLER'S THEORY AND CONCEPT OF TRAGEDY

MR. D. PRADEEK

ISBN 979-888569398-1

Contents

CHAPTER ONE

INTRODUCTION

Drama in the United States of America was always incapable of keeping pace with the progress in other branches of literature. Although by the nineteenth century, the puritan prejudice against theatre had completely vanished and great many plays had been produced, majority of the plays seldom transcended mediocrity. The people's need for drama was satisfied often by imported stuff.

The period preceding the end of the nineteenth century was a period of dearth in the history of English drama. The standards of drama has fallen and the theatre became impoverished. A sudden rival in drama took place with the contribution of G.B Shaw and many other Dramatist. But the American theatre was found, far behind the times. By the next decade playwrights became increasingly aware of the richness of American scene. Themes of wide interest and contemporary significances found their ways into the theater. The rise of the Little Theatre Movement marked in America the liberation of drama from conventional shackles imposed by the Commercial theatre. The Province-Town Players, a group of young artists and playwrights got dynamism from the leadership of O' Neil.

The Modern American Drama originated from the Little Theatre Movement in the second decade of the present century. Many theatre groups like Province Town Theatre, The New American Theatre, and The Neighbourhood Play -house were established. A school of writers sprang up, led by William Dunlop, probably the most prolific adapter of French and German plays in the nineteenth century.

The plays of Henrik Ibsen, Anton Chekhov, and August Strindberg came as a startling revelation to American playwrights, Ibsen and Shaw deeply influenced Modern American playwrights, particularly the young hopefuls longing for greater substance in the offerings of the American theatre. The social changes implied by Ibsen in, **A Doll's House, Hedda Gabler, The Wild Duck**, and **John Gabriel Borkman**, as well as his probing into character, served as a stimulus and challenge to fledgling dramatists eager to try their wings. The poet among these early figures in the American drama was William Vaughan Moody, whose principal theme was the conflict between Puritanism and Passion. In his verse dramas **The Faith Healer** and **The Great Divide**, he went one step farther than his colleagues in the search for truth. Young hands like Robert Edmond Jones, Lee Simonson, and Norman Bel Geddes created new physical settings for the life of the drama, which in turn gave rise to greater spiritual achievement. Finally there was a fresh approach, a changed order, and greater growth than the American theatre has shown for over half a century. The stage was set, the cue given and the modern playwrights promptly made their appearance. There raised individual dramatists like O' Neil, Tennessee Williams and Arthur Miller who had drawn up their own manifestoes of dramatic art.

O' Neil was the genius behind the change that came over the American theatre and made 1920's and 1930's the greatest period in its history. Post- dramatic scene was dominated by Tennessee Williams and Arthur Miller. Both the playwrights began to shine before the second World War. **The Glass Menagerie** by Williams and **All my sons** by Arthur Miller were plays of family tensions reflecting Contemporary American Society.

Miller and Williams had common ground to agree and share with each other. Both were against life printed on dollar bills. Both echoed the evils of American system of life. Their main theme was frustration and desperation. Though Miller and Williams look up the same theme, their techniques were different. A common characteristic feature of these two writers was their love for the bruised individual soul and the desperation of man. Arthur Miller was very much influenced by the Contemporary concern and American Dream. His radical views was against racism, capitalism and Vietnam War. All these ideas are amply reflected in his plays.

Miller has been one of the most outspoken American writers of last four decades. He was born in a middle class Jewish family in New York. He died on February 10, 2005. His father, Isadore Miller was a businessman. Family loyalty was strong among the Millers. Arthur Miller grew up a tall, gaunt, high school football star, but he was prevented from going to college because of the depression which affected his fathers business.

The Great Depression of the thirties in America was a tumultuous time when thousands of people found themselves poor all of sudden because of the economic crisis. Miller grew up through this period of his nation's crisis with a sharp sense of social injustice and degradation that came with the loss of moral values. In a speech ('The shadow of the Gods') delivered in 1958 to a gathering of new dramatists in New York, Miller describes his childhood and adolescence in the midst of the depression, and also the poverty of an early life which was forced upon him. It can easily be seen that the traumatic experience of sudden poverty coincided in Miller's life with his adolescence – an age which in any case brings disillusionment and knowledge as a part of the process of growing up. Miller talks repeatedly of the hidden forces of life which are stronger than individual mind's effort or will. What he means is that as in Greek tragedy, man is a victim of the forces which operate outside of his control and are generally at cross purpose to his own action and design.

According to Miller, such a force in Greek times may have been called mysterious fate or destiny, in modern times, it is the power of capitalism and the urbanized value system that tends to regiment and control the life of an average individual. After writing a few amateur stage-pieces during his college days, Arthur Miller began to write radio plays. But he did not relish writing for radio. The medium had too many taboos and restrictions, and its scripts had to be short and almost banally simple. Much of his work was done for 'The Cavalcade of America' and 'The Columbia Workshop'. Nevertheless, his career as a radio playwright in the forties provided him a kind of artistic discipline.

Robert Hogan says that some of his published plays show a freshness fairly rare for radio, and they help to repute the notion of Miller as totally humourless conscience of his race. Some of his well known radio scripts are **The Pussycat and the Expert Plumber who was a Man, A View from the Crucible** and **The Misfits**.

When World War II broke out, he did some scripts for a documentary film, the story of G.I. Joe, based on Ernie Pyle's Columns of the War. He also visited numerous army campuses and kept a record of them in his diary and later published these records under the title Situation Normal. He had also been working on a novel which was his protest against an openly Fascist organization, but disguised by the name Christian Front. Miller's book, **Focus**, revealed the Anti-Semitism of such organizations, and pointed to dangers of religious prejudice. It received notable coverage in the press, provoking varied opinion and discussion of its timely subject.

Miller suggests that the individual must protest against the injustice and the rigidity of society even at the cost of his life. Though Miller is apparently preoccupied with the individual and society, he betrays his metaphysical doubts. Eric Mottram says, Miller finally has come to believe that 'evil' is really the natural cruelty of human nature seen, not as a product of historical, social structures, but as inevitable data. The dilemma of his last two plays lies here in a nagging circularity which makes his work typical of frustrated American Liberalism. After Ibsen and Shaw, Miller is the only dramatist who has the ambition to write a mature drama which transcends the family crisis, sexual conflict and the individual psychosis.

Miller's first play to appear on Broadway was **The Man Who Had All the Luck** (1944). This lasted for only four performances. It deals with a young man in a small town who out of sheer luck gets what ever he wants. He owns several growing business, marries the girl he loves, begets a healthy child. As his desires are gratified, he is causing to accumulate around his own head an invisible but palpable fund, so to speak of retribution. As people are frustrated in one way or other he thinks, he too will be frustrated. He wails for some disaster to strike him but nothing happens. His friend fails simply through bad luck. The idea of an unseen fate guiding human destiny derives him mad, but he is happy the moment he thinks that his own ability and careful action are responsible for his success.

All My Sons (1947) is a play written for a prophetic theatre. Joe Keller makes profit by selling defective engines to the Air force directly causing their pilot's deaths. He allows his sub – ordinate, Deever to be imprisoned and disgraced for his own crime. His own son, Chris Keller, the returned Army officer, rejects his father. Chris and his mother condemn Keller's selfishness and point out to him that he should have regarded all young men as his sons. This sharp Criticism of Chris and Kate drive Keller to shoot himself dead. Through Chris, Miller expresses his view that a man is indebted more to society than to his family and that the welfare of society at large is more important than personal benefits.

The Crucible (1953) is Miller's most controversial play; it is based upon the witch trails held in Salem, Massachusetts, in 1952-53. The play is about John Proctor, who otherwise a good man, commits fornication. Abigail is the girl who seduces him and then black mails him. He confesses his son to his wife and earns her hatred and oldness. Abigail who wants to get Proctor's wife out of her way accuses her of witch craft. In the trail that follows Proctor is made to confess his guilt and gets disgusted. He attacks law and all authority, as a consequence of which he is executed.

A View from the Bridge (1956) is a history of Eddie Carbon, a civilian, who has an incestuous passion for his niece. He tries to prove that Rodalpho is a homosexual. By the accusation of homosexuality, he thinks of getting rid of Rodalpho. But the Sicilian law condemns Eddie's betrayal of honour. Now the tables are turned against Eddie. There is a fight between Marco, Rudolph's brother and Eddie in which Eddie is killed. The play shows how relentless pursuit of unrequited passion can destroy a man.

Miller's film script **The Misfits** (1961) is a powerful drama of the love of a woman for three delinquent men. The play unfolds the gutter life led by the three lonely men who are all bums. She is not able to form any meaningful relation with any one of them though in her company they become transformed from their animal level to loving human beings.

After the Fall (1964) is a play in which Miller comes to his theme of American success. It is also the author's self analysis, in a way. The play is addressed to an unseen listener. The depression, McCarthy trials, the disillusionment with socialist ideology and the broken marriages, all remind one of the marathon task that the playwright has taken upon himself. It is said that Maggie's character in the play was modeled on Marilyn Munroe. The play narrates the deterioration of Maggie's relation with Quentin, the hero of the play. Quentin and Maggie demand limitless love of each other and they fail to get it. Miller is painfully conscious of the alienation of the individual from an indifferent or unsympathetic society.

In **Incident at Vichy** (1964), Miller celebrates the strength of human dignity while continuing to examine the nature of deception and the limitations of personal guilt. This play, set in occupied France during World War II, features seven men who discuss their fate and the importance of social commitment in maintaining group freedom while awaiting interrogation by their Nazi captors.

Their conclusions suggest that those who fail to resist oppression are as guilty as the Nazis of crimes against humanity.

The Price (1968) is a realistic family drama in which two brothers, Victor and Walter, are brought together after many years by the death of their father. When Victor accuses his brother of abandoning their father during the Depression, Walter refuses to accept the burden of guilt, and the brothers' part in anger.

The Creation of the World and Other Business (1972), later revised under the title. **Up from Paradise**, is Miller's most radical deviation from his initial style. Written in a lightly humorous tone, this drama pits God against the devil in a debate concerning humanity's worth. This drama met with severe critical reprobation and closed after only twenty performances on Broadway.

The Archbishop's Ceiling (1977), set in a communist European Country, is an intellectual drama in which Miller celebrates the power of the human will. This play chronicles the artistic struggles of a dissident novelist who reacts to government censure by shunning exile and fighting for his freedom.

The American Clock (1980), structured as a series of Vignettes that Function as a social history of the United States, suggests that the hardship and suffering of the Depression served to unify and stronger American society.

Danger Memory (1987), consist of two one – act plays which explore the relationship of the past to the present.

Death of a Salesman (1949) is regarded as the finest of Miller's works. Willy Loman, the protagonist of this play, is also wrapped up in self delusions like Keller. He thinks that, with his personal attractiveness and pleasant social manners he is a most successful salesman. He is not aware of his limitations. But as the play progresses, his short – comings surface one by one. He loses his Job, discovers that his idealistic elder son is a failure and that his younger son, though successful in business, is morally rotten. Like Keller, Loman also commits suicide, as his dreams are shattered. It exposes the boastful, self made American businessman who cannot, however, stand a crisis.

Miller's reputation rests in large measure on the Pulitzer Prize Winning **Death of a Salesman**, a tragedy of the common man caught up in the false values imposed by middle – class American society. The play expresses his belief that the common man is a 'fit hero' for tragedy, that the tragic feeling is evoked (by) a character that is ready to lay down his life, if need be, to secure..... his sense of personal dignity. Like John Proctor in **The Crucible**, Willy Loman, the salesman protagonist, certainly conforms to this principle. Miller has also stated that the tragedian must believe in 'right way to live'. Whether this belief is to be retained by the dramatist or is to be explicitly worked into the drama is not clear; no 'right way' no nobler set of values, is offered in this play, except perhaps in Biff's conclusion that must recognize the 'truth' about oneself. Despite criticism leveled at the play's failure as a tragedy and its occasional tendency toward sentimental melodrama, it is undeniably a work of power.

Death of a Salesman is an instant success. It is hailed as a modern classic and has put Miller among the foremost playwrights. Miller is concerned with the theme of man being a victim of the evils of a commercial society. Though the individual is humanized in detail and depth, the ultimate feeling is that man is a victim of society, who is partially responsible for his own fate.

Willy Loman's, dreams and fantasies of success and wealth are accompanied by failure and disillusionment in his professional and private life. In his total commitment to the notion of 'selling' Willy kills himself in an auto accident, to achieve through death what he fails to achieve in life. Ironically he sells himself as a last resort.

Miller's recurring themes are the relationship of the individual to the society, the personal responsibility that the individual owes to society and the society failing the individual. 'Evil' is the outcome of the conflict between the social pressure and the individual's will to succeed. Miller tries to earn the sympathy of the audience for him and makes him a martyr to a false ethic of family and business sentimentality. **Death of a Salesman** can be interpreted as an indictment of the modern civilization to which millions of Loman are becoming daily victims. He breaks down the time and space sequences and creates the conflict between illusion and reality.

Miller occupies a fairly high place among the American writers of recent times. Miller's concept of drama is very clear when he wrote in his essay **Tragedy and the common Man** that tragedy stemmed from an attempt on the part of the protagonist to set right him or the society in which he is born. Another feature of Miller's plays is the emphasis on truth and morality. In short, he is a moralist and this naturally has raised a lot of opposition from his critics.

In his dramatic art Miller has experimented with various forms although a realistic representation of action has been the mainstay of his plays. Miller has openly recognized the limitations of realism which is associated with Ibsen and Shaw, and firmly believes that the requirements of the present day theatre demand a more liberated and effective mode than realism. The expressionistic and non – realistic technique used in plays like **Death of a Salesman** and **After the Fall** are sufficient evidence. The language of Miller's plays is colloquial, simple, direct and dramatic. His plays, besides being highly entertaining are rich in the dramatic content. But more than anything else, the intellectual appeal of his plays is very strong. He generally has the contemporary scene in mind even while writing about the myth of Adam and Eve.

Succeeding chapters are a study of Arthur Miller's theory and concept of tragedy, as projected in his play **Death of a Salesman**. Miller's tragic vision differs very much from the traditional view, and this project aims at bringing out the basic difference.

CHAPTER TWO

MILLER'S THEORY OF TRAGEDY

The subject of tragedy has been a perennial interest to mankind. The facts of tragedy have haunted the spirit of every man in all ages, and for this reason the subject of tragedy has usually interested those who feel the need for a more intelligent awareness of themselves and the world in which they live.

A large number of books and articles have appeared on tragedy giving widely different definitions. Arthur Miller has been seriously concerned with the study of the tragic mode.

Miller's approach to the subject has made him conscious of what he has done and what could be tried in the dramatic form. In trying to understand Millers theory of tragedy the key document is not only his well known essay **Tragedy and the Common Man** which appeared in the New York Times on February 29, 1949 two weeks after the opening performance of **Death of a Salesman**. But also his views in **TheIntroduction to the Collected Plays** in 1957. A number of interviews he gave from time to time also clarify some of his fundamental assumptions about tragedy. There is a continual process of growth, development and change in the ideas concerning tragedy.

For Miller the tragic phenomenon was an arena of near theological devout mess and he has set forth his views on the nature of tragedy and the tragic emotion. His reflections reveal him as a critic of particular strength and understanding.

Before discussing Miller's theory of tragedy it would be beneficial to keep in view some of the theories of tragedy before Miller. Since the earliest time of the classical Greeks, there has been a search for a definition of tragedy. The most influential earliest definition was of Aristotle in his Poetics.

Tragedy....... Is an imitation of an action that is serious, complete, and of a certain magnitude in language embellished with each kind of artistic ornament, the several kinds being found in separate parts of the play; in the form action not of narrative; through pity and fear effecting the proper purgation of these emotions (William. K. Wimsatt 36).

According to Aristotle the plot of a tragedy should be a whole. A whole is that which has a beginning, middle, and an end; a beginning is that which has nothing before it and an end is that which has nothing after it. A plot is casually a related sequence of events.

Aristotle's description of classical Greek tragedy provides insight into the genre. He defines the tragic hero as one of noble birth, who is neither all good nor all bad suffering a major reversal in fortune (peripeteia) due to a tragic flaw (hamartia) the tragic heroes learn from their downfall. He further pointed out that the classical tragedies focused on one main action.

A tragic event is one in which an individual suffers greatly, one in which he suffers self-consciously, is aware of his plight and perhaps learning from it; and one in which he struggles against his suffering and its causes. Tragedy, therefore, is "truer" than history in which things frequently happen by chance. As in a science fiction, everything should follow with reasonable probability, no matter how impossible those initial premises may be. The truth of tragedy is that it imitates the universal in the particular. It shows what history would be if there were no accidents. It imitates the true form of things, rather than their accidental appearance.

The second value of tragedy according to Aristotle, is that it makes one a better citizen; it has a moral effect. The key word here is Catharsis which means purgation; it is a medical term, and Aristotle applies it to the emotional release the audience gets from witnessing a tragedy. The specific emotions that aroused are pity and fear, which are purged or drained off so that the audience departs ready to face life again. Aristotle is directly answering Plato's charge that the tragedy stirs up a lot of undesirable emotions.

The final value of tragedy is its real purpose, which is pleasure. For some reason, not only the recognition of truth, but also the arousing and purgation of the emotions of pity and fear is pleasant; and this particular pleasure is what tragedy is for. Horace, in his **Art of Poetry** (24.20.B.c) also prescribed rules for tragedy. He stressed consistency in character and the exclusion of comic relief. He felt that the function of tragedy was to teach.

The Italian Renaissance critics like Julius Caesar Scaliger (1484-1558) and Lodovice Castelverto (1505-1571) gave some rigid criteria or tragedy. Their pronouncements were debated for centuries. For these critics, tragedy dealt with individuals of high birth. A mixture of genres was forbidden. The unities of time, place and action could not be violated. They indicated that the tragic playwright should strive for an illusion of reality or verisimilitude. They stressed the didactic aspect of tragedies.

In Elizabethan England, Sir Philip Sidney in **The Defense of Poesy** (1585) supported the Italian neo-classical ideals. During the Restoration period, John Dryden, in **An Essay of Dramatic Poesy** (1668) tried to balance the neo-classical ideals with the Elizabethan playwrights whose practice did not adhere to the neo-classical ideals with the Elizabethan playwrights whose practice did not adhere to the neo-classical ideals. In Spain, Lope de Vega defended his breaking of the neo-classical rules in his essay **The New Art of writing plays** (1609).

During the eighteenth century, there was a movement away from strict adherence to the Italian ideals. Dr. Samuel Johnson's **Preface to Shakespeare** (1765) is a defense of Shakespeare's tragic style. Gotthold Ephraim Lessing, in **Hamburg Dramaturgy** (1767-69) suggested that the neo-classical critics have misinterpreted Aristotle. He also called for critical acceptance of domestic tragedy, which dealt with nineteenth centuries, the German Romantics, among whom were Goethe and Friedrich Schiller, began writing tragedies that emulated Shakespeare rather than the Greeks. During the nineteenth century, philosophers attempted to determine the relation between tragedy and contemporary life.

During the twentieth century, writers have incorporated discoveries about ritual and other past theatrical practices into theories of Greek and Elizabethan tragedy. "Recent notions of the tragic universe suggest more comprehensive causes for the disorder reflected in these plays than a single factor, such as tragic flaw" (Dr. Usha Dutta 50).

The twentieth century has seen the breakdown of generic definitions and differentiations. This is indicated in George Steiner's book **The Death of Tragedy**(1961). Similarly the Swiss playwright Friedrich Duerrenmatt in **The Visit** (1956) has suggested that tragedy may no longer be possible in the "Punch and Judy show of our century" (Edwin Wilson 315).

The question that continues to disturb literary circles is whether it is possible to write tragedy in modern time. The subject has interested academic as well as non- academic critics and creative writers. They feel that the exalted art of tragedy, traditionally dealing with the fate of individual, is hard to flourish in the modern mechanical age.

The two well known authorities on this subject, Joseph Wood Krutch and Alan Renolds Thompson expressed the general consensus of opinion as now tragedy is impossible. Krutch in his essay **The Tragic Fallacy** in **The Modern Temper** (1929) despaired of the tragic fate, which had overtaken modern man. He felt that real tragedy had vanished with the great ages of the Greeks and Elizabethans. The world was a shrunken place losing its touch with the heroic. The modern vision was not ample and passionate as compared to Sophocles or Shakespeare. He felt that "God and Man and Nature had all somehow dwindled in the course of the intervening centuries" (Joseph Wood Krutch 81). A tragic writer according to Krutch "does not have to believe in God, but he must believe in man" (81).

Thompson in the **Anatomy of Drama** (1946) announced that tragedy in the classical tradition sustained the faith in mankind as it was heroic. He felt that in the modern age "the spirit of the time itself has run counter to the heroic tradition" (292). Modern democracy, commercialism, science psychology have all influenced the modern writer of tragedy who finds himself in a dilemma, "unable to believe in greatness, he cannot inspire others. If he would gain elevation, he must falsify his beliefs; if he would express his candid view of life he must forego the tragic lift" (292). It is that the heroic tragedy was the outcome of a pessimistic view about things in general, but was optimistic about virtue in the individual. The modern view tends to be pessimistic about everything and hence there is no possibility of heroism.

The opinion that no true tragedy can be produced in modern times has continued to disturb many minds. John Lewis Longley pinpointed the modern dilemma in **The Tragic Mask** (1963) by saying that "man has such an abysmal estimate of himself that even if a writer could be found to produce a tragedy, no one would take it seriously" (167).

Since there is no generally accepted and acceptable definition of tragedy, Miller is fascinated by the difficult problem of defining the genre. He looks at the problem from a practical rather than a theoretical angle. Miller while declaring that few tragedies are written in the modern age also points out that the fault lies not with the writer but the times. He feels that what tragedy requires of the artist first and of the audience thereafter is kind of grief without which the tragic area somehow cannot be approached. Instead of grief we have come to substitute irony and even comedy. Claiming that the whole ritual of showing and sharing grief has been misplaced he extends the causes of lack of tragedy to the waning influence of organized religion and to the many revolutions man has passed through like the Nazi Holocaust.

It modern times "the tragic proposal is simply presumptuous - thus making so much out of one death when we know it is meaningless. In other words, in an important respect we have ceased to feel" (Arthur Miller 212). Thus Miller feels that the previous cries against heaven or fate have come to be stylized only with a "grin" or a "cough". The modern literature takes a purely psychological or purely sociological view of tragedy. Miller has a strong conviction that because tragedies are still responded today as the earlier times, they are vital for man. This also affirms his faith in the existence of the tragic sense and the tragic art in modern times.

To understand the growth in Miller's critical thought one must first turn to his essay, **Tragedy and the Common Man** (1949) published immediately after the opening of **Death of a Salesman**, Miller defends the 'common man' as a suitable hero for tragedy. It was Aristotle, first, who discussed the nature of tragic hero and much subsequent criticism centers on the point. The hero, according to Aristotle must be one who is highly renowned and prosperous personages like Oedipus, Thyestes or other illustrious men of such families. The theatre and dramatic theory for long supported this judgment. In 1536 Danielo declared that while comedy dealt with domestic stuff, tragedy dealt with deaths of high kings and ruins of great empires. Influential critics like Scalinger and Castelvetro, agreed that "the actions of kings are the subject of tragedy" (Dr. Usha Dutta 54).

It was Friedrich Hebbel who showed the connection between tragedy and the average man. Eric Bentley in **The Playwright as Thinker** mentioned "one need only be a man, after all, to have a destiny" (31). If Bucher was the first dramatist of the little man in his tragedy **Woyzeck**, it was Hebbel who advocated the middle class man in which Ibsen later found the symbol of modern society and era. For Ibsen the character of the average man is in no way trivial from the artistic standpoint; as an artistic reproduction it is as interesting as any other. Miller in his theory goes beyond Lillo in asserting that the problems of monarchy are of no interest at all. "The right of one monarch to capture the domain from another no longer raises our passions, nor are our concepts of justices what they were to the mind of an Elizabethan king" (Arthur Miller 5).

The most controversial statement of Miller was in his **TheatreEssay Tragedy and the Common Man.**

I believe that the common man is an apt a subject for tragedy in its higher sense as kings were. On the face of it this ought to be obvious in the light of modern psychiatry, which bases its analysis upon classic formulations, such as Oedipus and Orestes complexes, for instances, which were enacted by royal beings, but which apply to everyone in similar emotional situations (3).

He further felt that the insistence upon the rank of the tragic hero was like clinging to the outward qualities of tragedy. His concern is the non - aristocratic tragic hero and not for the Aristotelian hero. Miller's theory of the common man has thus succeeded in recognizing explicitly the aesthetic problem. It also seeks an answer in affective response. Miller has worked from the traditional definition and improved it rather than starting afresh.

In his essay on **Tragedy and the Common Man**, Miller states that the tragic hero is "ready to lay down his life, it need be, to secure one thing - his sense of personal dignity ... the underlying struggle is that of the individual attempting to gain his 'rightful' position in the society" (4). Miller is concerned with the basic problem of the individual in his society and feels that tragedy is the consequence of man's total compulsion to evaluate himself justly, "his destruction in the attempt posits a wrong or evil in his environment"(5). Such statement taken out of context have tempted critics to call Miller a social determinist who sees man as victim of the society.

Critics like Eric Bentley felt that the tragedy and social drama actually conflict. But it is John Gassner who came with an opposite point of view with the question why indeed can not 'Social Drama' be tragedy? He feels social drama can also rise to the heights of tragedy, if the protagonist looms humanly large among his fellow-creatures of the play and if his value, however deplorable in their particular results, magnify rather than diminish him as human being" (John Gassner 21). If the sympathies of the author are with the common man and not primarily in social causation it can be a tragedy. A playwright with enough intelligence and talent can stress on humanity rather then history.

It is with the **Introduction to the Collected Plays** that Miller's views gain weight. He feels that if a writer is to reflect reality he must depict why a man acts in a typical manner and why he cannot simply walk away without acting the way he did, "for in truth there are an extraordinary small number of conflicts which must, at any cost, live out to their conclusions"(117).

Here Miller goes beyond the requirements of the 'tragic law' in the Poetics. Since the character seems to question the stable environment, the importance of the tragic flaw gains measure. For Miller, the tragic flaw is not necessary a weakness but is man's unwillingness to remain passive when his right and dignity are challenged. Only the passive, for Miller, are flawless. Thus the accepted notion of the tragic flaw as a shortcoming in the hero is transformed by Miller into what seems a condition of greatness in the hero. The writer has to probe deeper for values and seek an insight into the cause of the actions of the hero.

Miller feels that "if one could know enough about a human being one could discover some conflict, some value, some challenges which he cannot find it in himself to walk away from or turn his back on" (118). This is the vital question to be solved by tragedy in every age.

Miller mentions Orestes, Hamlet, Medea and Macbeth, and thus seems to be affirming continuity in tragedy that is not dependent upon historical accidents. What matters is the tragic sense, not the mechanical outward details of an abstract formula for the tragic. As a critic Miller is perceptive to see the significance of the **Death of a Salesman** in line with Sophocles' **Electra** or Shakespeare's **Hamlet**. The very fact that Miller sees a common thread in the tragic visions of the above writers indicates the extents to which his imagination breaks through the barriers of literary genres, movements and periods.

Miller's views seem to confirm Murray Kreiger's definition of tragedy and tragic vision. The most obvious difference according to Krieger between the two is a crucial one:

"*Tragedy*" refers to an object's literary form, the "*tragic vision*" to a subject's psychology, his view and version of reality. Perhaps it would be more accurate to say that the tragic vision was born inside tragedy, as a part of it: as a possession of the tragic hero, the vision was a reflection in the realm of thematics of the fully fashioned aesthetic totality which was tragedy. But fearful and even demoniac in its revelations, the vision needed the ultimate soothing power of the aesthetic form which contained it –a tragedy itself – in order to preserve for the world a sanity which the vision itself denied (Krieger 23).

The tragic vision in Miller has power to see Oedipus' quest to the moment of destruction, Macbeth's road to disaster, Willy's drive to insanity in the nature of the character's conflict. For Miller the less capable a man is of walking away from the central conflict of the play, the closer he approaches a tragic existence. In turn, this implies that the closer a man approaches tragedy; the more intense is his concentration of emotion upon the fixed point of his commitment.

For Miller, the hero has to face his challenge and his dilemma as he is a person of intensity. He has to follow his path with emotional and intellectual nature to fullness. He cannot leave it half way or turn his back. Also, the commitment to his cause is so intense and fundamental, that he prefers to face death rather than relinquish it. The word commitment itself, in modern usage, carries philosophical and religious overtones that are important. One might say that, among other things, a commitment involves the notion of a personal free act by which an individual makes a decisive choice. His subsequent mode of being and acting are somehow affected by this act.

Miller, having established the necessity for the heroes' basic awareness in his Introduction approaches the problem of nobility or stature as an extension of his earlier discussions. Firstly, he feels that stature should not be confused with rank. Today, the hero has alternatives to materially change the course of his life and in this respect "he cannot be debarred from the heroic role" (Miller 145). Thus the stress is on the action of sufficient magnitude to change the character's life.

Secondly, to this action Miller adds intensity of the hero's commitment. The magnitude of a grocer's stature is not reduced in comparison to a President's provided the values that are implied are of equal measure. This is possible Miller feels if the issues involved are "the survival of the race, the relationships of man to God, in short, whose answers define humanity and the right way to live so that the world is a home, instead of a battleground or a fog in which disembodied spirits pass each other in an endless twilight" (145).

Another aspect stressed by Miller in his "Introduction" is the process of man's efforts to evaluate him justly. This is for the discovery of the moral law in the universe. It is on the basis of the writer's personal view of reality that he builds the conflict within his characters. For Miller, tragedy must question everything and man is always in the process of becoming and being shaped. Man is not seen as a private entity by Miller nor are his social relations merely thrown at him. He sees society as inside man and man inside society.

The genuine conflicts of the hero which Miller builds up in his plays involve the real questions of right and wrong of free will and of choice and responsibility. Miller here touches metaphysical levels, not as a philosopher but as an artist. He tries for the tragic effect by bringing out timeless implications. Miller in the age of the common man shows man's demand for recognition of his individuality and mobility of spirit.

Miller has frankly admitted that "The longer I dwelt on the whole spectacle; the clearer becomes the failure of the present age to find a universal moral sanction" (160). But for Miller tragedy was the only important form, tragedy was the basic pillar. He does not take man to regions of philosophy and metaphysics for their own sake. He does not try to solve the problems of the common man, yet as a playwright and in his essays he has shown that he is aware of the problems. As a dramatic critic he knows that no direct or arithmetical comparison can be made between contemporary work and classical tragedies. In the present age where man struggles amid difficult environment, the individual is given a heroic stature by Miller, raising him above the helpless crowds.

As a dramatist Miller builds his conflict on the commitment of his heroes to their cause, their set of values. To the end, Willy is faithfully committed to his dream, his false dream of success. Some critics have stressed that in a tragedy the main character must reach perception. For Maxwell Aderson the central experience of tragedy is the main character's discovery of something important, about him or about the world, that changed him to a better person. But Miller, according to his theory thought it more important to show Willy steadfast in his commitment, happy in his death rather than to show him realizing that his whole life had been a mistake. Willy is committed to his dream and dies for it. The other characters of course gain perception and clarify the issue.

Miller, in his plays and essays in some respects does show adherence to the classical notions of death. He declared that he could not separate tragedy from death in his mind. He knew there was no reason to put these together but felt that "there's nothing like death. Dying isn't like it you know. There's no substitute for the impact on the mind of the spectacle of death. And there is no possibility; it seems to me, of speaking of tragedy without it" (266). Since everything occurs for Miller through the past and present, the lasting appeal of tragedy is

Due to our need to face the fact of death in order to strengthen ourselves for life, and that over and above this function of the tragic viewpoint there are and will be a great number of formal variations which no single definition will ever embrace (Miller 146).

Another key idea in Miller's theory of tragedy is the stress on the effect of drama. It was Aristotle who of soul by 'pity' and 'fear'. Gassner in **Tragedy in Modern Theatre** declared that "Each age has added its own interpretation, naturally reflecting its own interests and its own kind of drama" (51).

Thus for Aristotle it was fear and pity, Clifford Leach in his **Shakespeare's Tragedies** (1950), declared it as terror and pride; Others will speak of sorrow and pain, of awe and understanding. Shakespeare himself seems to have thought in terms of woe and wonder; some modern critics have stressed good and evil or have developed the antithesis in a psychological manner.

Miller in his theory returns to a more classic type of tragedy involving the audience not only emotionally but also intellectually. Much the same view has been expressed by such modern critics as Francis Fergusson, Kenneth Burke, and John Gessner. All agree that tragedy must terminate in knowledge. For Miller enlightenment should not end in an attack on the audience's nerves and feelings only. The end of tragedy must take place in the consciousness of the beholder.

Miller is also aware that the playwrights of the thirties did not lay stress on character but on their preconceived scheme of how dreadful the world was-the character had no importance, he started without enlightenment and he ended with some kind of enlightenment. It is in this context that Miller's theory of tragedy and enlightenment gain momentum and importance

Miller, like most tragedians is seeking a new explanation of the human situation with its tragic aspects. He however seeks it in humanistic terms not transcendal ones. If the mechanistic environment restricts hampers and defeats us, then it can be changed as one's wish. The modern dramatist should show not only defeat but also a free will. Miller feels that even if the external factors are the source of making man a victim, he can, if he resists his environment or fate in order to change it.

Thus the underlying position in Miller is optimistic and not pessimistic. This gain sets him apart from playwrights and critics who associate pessimism with tragedy. In his interview with Philip Gelb, **Morality and Modern Drama** he declared that he could not write when he was unhappy. "A lot of writers write best when they are most miserable. I suppose my sense of form comes from a positive need to organize life and not from a desire to demonstrate the inevitability of defeat and death" (208).

It seems no more proper to see Miller's criticism in the light of his play than to see his plays in the light of his theory. Yet the great traditional examples of dramatic theory like Aristotle's **Poetics**, Dryden's **Essay of Dramatic Poesy**, and Coleridge's **Shakespearean Criticism** were all written after the works; they all like Miller had proved the power of criticism to move and clarify. W. H. Auden in an essay (1945) remarked how at the end of a Greek play audience say "What a pity it had to be this way" while at the end of a "Christian tragedy they say what a pity it had to be this way when it might have been otherwise" (91).

The distinction stresses the difference between the two cultures, whereas in Greek drama the sense of fate rules, residing in forces outside man, in the Christian tragedy a sense of greater personal freedom is implied in man is free to act morally. Arthur Miller combines both. In Christian drama the situation is not given, but as in Greek drama the forces making for tragedy are often outside the protagonist- he is caught in circumstances not of his own making. But unlike Greek Drama, these are the forces that determine the fate of the protagonist that are not beyond his reach. Hence the possibility of decisive action is held out, and the will of the hero is brought into the play.

Critics are puzzled with the question whether Miller is having a loose or a very clear theory of tragedy, whether he is classical, tradition bound or modern, the answer perhaps lies in the type of analysis that Robert Hogan provides. He mentions two tragic traditions in the western world the austere and the experimental structure wise he places Euripides, Shakespeare, O'Casey, and Tennessee Williams in one tradition and Sophocles, Racine, Ibsen and Arthur Miller in another. Yet the plays of Miller have more than a merely structural similarity to those earlier men, "Miller's also vitally embody the austere tragic spirit. That embodiment, in a time which is overwhelmingly eclectic and experimental, gives the real meaning and the real importance to the works of Arthur Miller" (Robert Hogan 6).

Miller balances his theory of tragedy between the old and the New concepts. He endeavours to create a drama equal in intensity to tragedy, drawing from tradition and also utilizing it in some fresh fashion. Miller's theory is specially important because it has grown out of his major strength as a playwright, his plays retaining permanent, universal themes. Though his theory is different from the classics in some respects, it is a classic one of American culture.

Miller has also with his theory placed himself squarely in this realistic tradition. For him drama is akin to the other inventions of man in that it ought to help one to know more, and not merely to spend his feelings. Every genuine new form of the drama makes possible a "new and heightened consciousness... of causation in the light of known but hither to inexplicable effects" (Dr. Usha Dutta 75). And Miller too rediscovers the historical function of the modern dramatist.

A new poem on the stage is a new concept of relationships between the one and many and history, and to create it requires greater attention, not less, to the inexorable, common, pervasive conditions of existence in this time and this hour (75).

Thus a historian, the dramatist perceives the social situation, and more narrowly the physical milieu as the condition of a tragic action. It is seen that from Hebbel to Miller, there is a distinct tradition of realistic tragic writing which conceives of the individual as a protagonist with a will of his own, which in other words, allows for the interplay between, historical necessity and individual freedom. Yet also in this respect the difference remains absolute between the old drama and the new; the hero in new drama is the representative of a moment in history and a distinct stratum of society, whereas the Greek or Shakespearean hero symbolizes the human condition in a timeless context of universal powers.

Miller is surely not one of those who claim that there is no modern tragedy, or that tragedy is dead. He is not among the thoughtful like George Steiner who gave the verdict that the death of God means the death of tragedy. If the fact that faith in God has been replaced by faith in man then Miller's theory encompasses and ensures faith in man. His theory reasserts his belief in the existence of tragedy.

Miller rejects the Greek Tragedy and calls it archaic, fit only for very highly placed personifications like Kings.

Then Miller proves that the common man is apt subject for tragedy, for exaltation of tragic action is a property off all man. The tragic feeling is aroused in the audience not by the stature of a hero but by his willingness to lay down even his life, to secure one thing with his sense of personal dignity. Tragedy then is the consequence of man's total compulsion to evaluate him or the individual attempting to gain his rightful position in his society. The feeling of terror and fear can be aroused by man's fight against the environment too. The tragedy of monarchs and royal persons would arouse much sympathy now as it did during the Elizabethan period. The tragedy implies more optimism in its author than the comedy, and that its final result ought to be the reinforcement of the onlooker's brightest opinion of the human animal. Tragedy takes place when a human being loses the grip of the force of life. Tragedy is a manifestation of truth according to Miller's theory.

CHAPTER THREE

"DEATH OF A SALESMAN" WITH REFERENCE TO MILLER'S THEORY OF TRAGEDY

Death of a Salesman is one of the best American plays. It may be more demonstrably flawed than its closest rivals, but it is a much richer play with more range and more resonance. It is also more of a public play and probably the only successful twentieth century tragedy with a hero whose heroism cannot be doubted.

In 1949 Willy Loman, riding on "a smile and a shoeshine" (Arthur Miller 105) and determined to be not just liked but well liked, made his way into American consciousness in **Death of a Salesman.** Miller wrote the play in six weeks, and for the first time in Brodway history, a play made a clean sweep of the top three awards. It won the triple crown of theatrical artistry that year: the Pulitzer Prize, the New York Drama Critics' Circle Award and the

Tony.

This play can be considered as a study of man's search for merit and worth in his life and his struggle against Contemporary American Society. Set within the family of the title character, Willy Loman, the play hinges on the uneven relationships of father and sons, husband and wife. It is a mirror of the literary attitudes of the 1940's, with its rich combination of realism tinged with naturalism; carefully drawn, rounded characters; and insistence; on the values of the individual, despite failure and error.

As a modern tragedian, Miller looks to the Greeks for inspiration, particularly Sophocles. From Orestes to Hamlet, Medea to Macbeth, the underlying struggle was that of the individual attempting to gain his rightful position in his society. Miller considers the common man "as apt a subject for tragedy in its highest sense as Kings was" (Arthur Miller 5). It tells the story of Willy Loman, an aging salesman who makes his way "on a smile and a shoeshine" (105). Miller lifts Willy's illusions and failures, his anguish and his family relationship, to the scale of a tragic hero. The fear of being displaced or having the image of what and who are destroyed is best known to the common man, Miller believes it is time that the modern age, which is without kings, took up this bright thread of history and followed it to the only place it can possibly lead in the present time - the heart and spirit of the average man.

In **Death of Salesman**, Miller comes closer to his theory of tragedy. The tragic scale is achieved by finding dignity in the struggle of the little man. Between the two world wars the little man had become the butt of jokes.

Harold Lloyd was one of the most popular comic little men, winning the girl or the ball game when some one else made a more stupid mistake and Charlie Chaplin immortalized the 'little fellow' with the sentiment and pathos of his clowning. In the twenties and thirties, patronizing contempt was a common attitude towards these lost souls of the cities. But when **Death of a Salesman** appeared in 1949, it was evident that a more serious attitude was possible. Postwar audiences were ready to believe that an ordinary man might suffer deeply and struggle with dignity (George R. Kernodle 219-220).

Willy makes a commitment to a set of values which are false. Miller finds appropriate concrete symbols for social realities of his time and place and also shows universal psychological conflicts within the American family. On the social level, Willy is a victim of the American dream, and this is personified in three different figures. In Ben, readers see the self made man who came out as rich from the jungle, Dave Singleman lived in strange cities and built his fame and fortune, and Willy's father was a creator who made flutes and high music.

Miller regarded **Death of a Salesman** always as heroic and the charge that Willy Loman lacked 'stature' for the tragic hero seemed unbelievable to him. Willy Loman is merely a middle class salesman. Thus he belongs to the common people who are almost in a common place. It should, however, be pointed out that **Death of a Salesman** was world - wide appeal. Two flaws of modern life are exposed by Miller. The first flaw is the nervous breakdown caused by an acquisitive civilization sans ideals. Willy Loman, the salesman, represents the modern man who places little value on spiritual ideals. This should make it absolutely clear that Miller doesn't have in mind any parallel such as King Lear, though Paul N. Siegel Hazards suggests such a connection between Willy Loman and King Lear. Willy is placed on a par with King Lear from the philosophical point of view, namely 'Know thyself '; Siegel also bases his conclusion on the fact that Willy Loman like King Lear evokes not merely pity but fear. This view is counter to the view of Eric Bentley.

Willy is a salesman in his late sixties. He cannot travel far and wide. He requests his master Howard to give him a sedentary job in the local office. But Howard takes exception to Willy's inability to travel and sacks him at once. Dejected, Willy goes to the restaurant where his sons Biff and Happy have arranged a party to celebrate the business in sporting goods which they propose to start with a massive loan from Biff's former employer Bill Oliver. Oliver is not interested in Biff's business plan. He refuses even to meet Biff. Biff leaves the restaurant abruptly because he does not have the courage to face his father. Happy also deserts his father whom he derisively calls 'this guy' and runs after two call – girls.

Linda is disgusted with her son's irresponsible ways and calls them 'animals' and 'scum'. She shows Biff a rubber tube in the cellar and explains to him that Willy is planning to commit suicide. But tells his father that it was because he attached excessive importance to his sporting prowess that he (Biff) has become very arrogant and incapable of taking orders from anybody. He asks his father to burn out his dreams and face the sordid reality that they are both very ordinary people. Biff cries and leans on his father, Willy is touched by Biff's love and dependence on him. He wants to help Biff to start a business. The problem is – how to raise the funds necessary for floating a company? Willy drives his car at terrific speed and kills himself in the hope that the insurance company will release twenty – thousand pounds to Biff with which he can improve his life. At the funeral all people forgive Willy, his failings and glorify him. Into this main plot is woven the sub – plot of Willy's reminiscences about Biff's greatness as a foot – ball player at school and Willy's brother Ben's meteoric rise as owner of diamond mines in Africa.

Willy Loman's values are very much those of contemporary society-the American Dream which the rest of the world mimics - and his downfall derives both from his personal failure in relation to his values and from the failure of the values themselves. The fluidity Miller contrives is such that he can sometimes make great capital out of the speed at which Willy's mind oscillates between past and present. For example, in the scene when Willy's dead brother Ben appears to him, he is conversing partly with the real man and partly with the image in his mind.

Willy : I'm getting awfully tired, Ben.

Charley : Good keep playing: you'll sleep better.

Did you call me Ben?

Willy : That's funny. For a second there you reminded me of my brother Ben (Miller 28-29).

At the beginning of the play the scene between Biff and Happy in the bedroom is interrupted by the scene between Willy and Linda in the kitchen. Both give us plenty of pointers to Willy's state of near breakdown. He has come back early from a Journey, finding that he cannot keep his mind on his driving. His mind goes blank of moments and is full of dreams and strange thoughts.

Willy's opinions and feelings are self - contradictory. He even contradicts himself verbally within a short time:

Willy

:

Biff is a lazy bum!

Linda

:

They're sleeping, Get something's to eat. Go on down

Willy

:

Why did he come home? I would like to know what brought him home.

Linda

:

I don't know. I think he's still lost, Willy. I think' he's very lost (5).

He goes on talking to himself as the lights come up on the boy's bedroom and we see them listening anxiously to the noise he is making and discussing his mental state. It bridges very effectively the present with the past, which is acted out and it shows the happiness of a frictionless family group, the sons proud of their father, the father proud of his sons.

Another aspect of Willy's personality is revealed. Apart from the above mentioned instances of unusual behaviour, Willy suffers from an acute sense of loneliness at his two sons not living with him any more. In spite to this grief Willy displays pride and affection for his son, Biff, whose childhood days he remembers with warmth.

Linda's character in the first scene is sharp contrast to that of Willy. She is an ideal wife, who loves and admires her husband. She has a sort of native and earthy wisdom which gives her strength to remain cool in all circumstances. Linda's care and affection make a tired Willy acknowledge her strength in these words:

Willy : You're my foundation and my support, Lind (7).

Throughout the play Linda is trying to hold the family together by acting as a common bond between Willy and his sons. It may be correctly assumed that Biff and Happy personify the two alternatives of Willy's dream of happiness. Biff carries out the pastoral happiness experiment and Happy lives out the idea of instant success.

As Linda is reassuring Willy that there is nothing wrong with him, another memory cuts across Willy's mind ands thus, there is a signal for a change of scene. In a short passing scene, Willy is shown with a woman with whom he is joking. Then, they stay in a hotel room. It is one of Willy's regular tours. The idea is to reveal ironically that Willy cheats his wife and that he gets very lonely and depressed.

Miller views Willy's situation as not merely the private dilemma of an individual, but the case history of common man and his predilections in general. Linda goes on to explain that Willy is simply an exhausted man. Willy continues to dream about the impending change, especially because he thinks that his son Biff has been reconciled to him. In spite of these being a climate of optimism, Miller uses this scene to highlight the vicious circle in which man is caught and the exploiting commercialism of modern society.

Linda reports about the pending bills to be paid for repairs to the car, refrigerator etc., and the last mortgage payment on the house. Willy curses the commercial exploitation of which he is a victim.

Willy : I'm always in a race with the junkyard (51).

But, ironically, it is the commercial values of his society - appearance, instant success etc, which gives Willy the sustenance's of his life. Anyway, his mood is softened by the information that his sons have invited him to dinner that evening in a restaurant.

The crucial thing about Willy's circumstances is that in the face of failure and a growing sense of his own inadequacies, he has transferred all his hopes and ambitions to his son Biff. Even Linda, when Biff calls on the telephone, declares:

Linda : Biff, you'll save his life (100).

Thus, Biff becomes a Symbol of Willy's hope of success and ultimately it is only in Biff's failure that Willy recognizes his own failure before he ends his life.

One of the ways of understanding **Death of a Salesmen** is to study it as the story of an innocent man made a victim by the selfish and harsh society. Willy's meeting with his employer enforces this aspects of the play in which Miller's sociological concerns are brought forth.

Willy pleads and argues with Howard for a permanent posting in New York so that he may not have to travel. He tries all the tricks to convince Howard, but to no avail. At this point in their discussion Willy narrates the story of Dave Singleman, the ideal salesman. It was Dave Singleman's life that had inspired Willy to become a salesman.

Willy : I realize that selling was the greatest career a man could want (57).

This is why Willy's confession of a total commitment to the values of a commercial and capitalistic society. Actually, Willy tells this story with a purpose, which is to express in his own way his sense of failure and his knowledge that the world and its values have changed from what he believed them to be five years ago.

Willy

:

There was respect, and comradeships and gratitude in it. Today, it's all cut and dried, and there's no chance for bringing friendship to bear - or personality (57-58)

It is when all appeals fail and when Howard does not want to listen to Willy any more, that Willy makes the well known outburst which sums up man's helplessness and his exploitation at the hands of a selfish society.

Willy

:

I put thirty - four years into this firm, Howard, and now I can't pay my insurance. You can't eat the orange and throw the peel away -a man is not a piece of fruit (58).

These lines from the play became hallmark of the postwar era. It is this orange - peel theory of Miller, which has led critics to believe that Willy Loman is a sociological tragedy showing man as a victim of an indifferent society. However, as Miller has himself clarified in the **Introduction to Collected Plays**, the play is a psychological tragedy also in which certain aspects of Willy's character also contribute to his downfall.

Willy bellowed coming to grips with the fact that he was no longer the hotshot salesman he once was and findings himself pleading with his young boss to keep his job, saying. "A man is not a piece of fruit" (58). Willy has told Howard that he has sacrificed a chance to go to Alaska with his brother. There, follows a 'Memory' scene with Ben. Ben clearly makes an offer to Willy to come along with him as there will be endless – opportunities. Willy is much tempted and almost willing, but it is Linda who throws cold water on this idea. Actually, Linda is revealed in this scene in a disappointing light though, her affection and concern for Willy remains unquestioned. But, she is shown as a woman of limited imagination, who values the dull middle class security of her present existence more than the promised but risky wealth of Alaska. She also reminds Willy of his hero, Dave Singleman; who has succeeded as a salesman. Linda uses every possible weapon to light off Ben's tempting offer.

Linda : why must everybody conquer the world? (61).

Willy fails to recognize in this statement a direct negation of all his ambitions and a close opportunity of realizing them is lost. By way of defending his inability to accept Ben's offer Willy falls back upon his false theory of the worth of appearance as compared to deeds. To illustrate his theory, he points to his son Biff who is ready to go and play a foot ball match

Willy

:

Without a penny to his name, three great universities are begging for him, and from there the sky's the limit, because it's not what you do, Ben. It's who you know and the smile on your face (61-62).

It is generally believed that Ben symbolises Willy's dream of success and riches. Biff tries to correct himself and improve but, he is disillusioned about his father. It is after this discovery that Biff throws away his chance to re-appear in the exam and, thus, ruin his life. It is as if the destruction of Willy's image in Biff's mind had automatically sealed his own fate.

Biff, however, is determined to have a frank talk with Willy before he leaves. He finds Willy in the backyard carrying a flash light, a hole and seeds. He is also talking to an imaginary Ben. It is obvious that Willy has finally decided to kill himself. He talks Ben of his insurance policy - which after his death will bring twenty thousand dollars to his family. Willy never succeeded in getting rich in his life, Willy became rich in death. As a salesman, he will sell the last thing he has - himself. When Ben tries to suggest that killing himself would be a cowardly act, Willy resorts:

Willy

:

Does it take more guts to stand here the rest of my life ringing up a zero? (94).

Already, he can visualize his funeral, which would be grand and befitting his status as a famous rich man. A man has got to add up something he feels that, his mind is made up of only regret which seems to be that he couldn't win his son's love. Therefore, when Biff seeks him out for frank talk, there follows a bitter quarrel, but at the end of which Willy learns that he can die with satisfaction in his heart.

Willy's notions of bigness and his silly dreams. He declared that he is a bum and not a special of all American heroes, as his father regards him to be

Ben: Pop I'm a dine a dozen, and so are you (99).

In his opinion, everyone in the Loman family lives by lies and sooner they wake up to reality, the better it will be for them. No one amongst the Loman's is great or extraordinary. They are ordinary, common people and must live and must accept the fate of all common people. All the dreams of riches and success are sources of trouble and make them dishonest.

Miller puts a lot of punch in Biff's analysis, whose attitude represents the inheritable defeat and capitulation of the common man. Willy, however, thinks that his son is behaving bitterly, because of his hatred for Willy. But Biff, at the height of his emotional outburst, breaks down into weeping and embraces Willy, who realizes that his son loves him and perhaps loved him all along. Immediately he falls back on his dreams of Biff's greatness. At the same time, a strange calm downs upon Willy, who goes out to kill himself in a car crash with contentment that he is reconciled to his son whom the insurance money will bring about a change for the better.

The brief "Requiem" shows the Loman family and Charley paying their homage to Willy. Linda, with full of remorse, does not understand why Willy killed himself. Biff blames Willy for having the wrong dreams and is ready to go away on his wanderings. Happy is determined to carry on his struggle to realize Willy's dream of success. Charley's comment is the most meaningful in which he understands that Willy was the product of a commercial society and he could not help being a salesman. A salesman, according to Charley.

Charley : A Salesman is got to dream boy (105).

It is this description of Willy which makes him a universal character. However, what Miller really wants to mean in Willy is, the reader should see the magnificent failure of the American story of success of the debilitating effect of the mechanization and a permissive society, with its cumulative ill effects. This is what typifies of America today. Miller's conception gains the added force, when one sees the dark alleys in the personal life of Willy, his affair with a sturdy woman in Boston and the broken home as evidenced by the rebellious attitude of his sons, Biff and Happy. Biff is a chip of the block, a vulgar immortal. He does his acts with impurity, because his father has no morals. He has even the gumption tell in the very face of his father, that he is a flake. The most intense scene comes when Willy is shattered in the Boston hotel room by Biff. Willy's reaction is his desperate attempts to restore his self image.

Unfortunately Willy has no courage to disown his rebellious sons. Paternal love stands in his way of reaping the little success that he could have despite the innumerable failures of his life. In other words, conscience has made a coward of Willy. It is this weakness in his character that makes him worry about the future of his sons Willy, thus, lives in a half - way house and proves to be a through failure in life. But, he makes ample for his lapses by his heroic and dying in a car smash. He does it deliberately, so that he could leave behind something for his wife and children to fall back on. Linda correctly assesses his character. Biff himself admits in the Requiem scene that his father 'had the wrong dream' Charley sums up the life of Willy to bring out his character effectively.

Charley

:

Willy was a salesman. And for a salesman, there is no rock bottom to the life ...He is a man out there in the blue, riding on a smile and a shoe shine. And when they start not smiling back - that's an earthquake ... No body dast blame this man (105).

The points raised by Miller in favour of **Death of a Salesman** being a tragedy are quiet convincing. As a critic of his own drama, Miller displays a sense of objectivity and astuteness, which is rather uncommon among other writer's. Miller states, in the Introduction, that **Death of Salesman** grew out of the images of loss, futility, bareness, sterility and aging. In one sense, Willy's life is tragic, because he has gone through the loss implied in the simple process of growing old. On the last day of his life, he is a sad and dejected old man, rejected by his sons and the rest of the world. His life is surrounded by images of broken things. Broken, things refrigerator belt, broken washing Machine, broken car, etc ... what is more, he has experienced 'broken' relationship with his sons and his employer. Thus, although Miller makes us believe the play to be positive in its effect, the overwhelming sense of loss is an essential ingredient of tragedy which cannot be ignored for Miller, Willy was agonized by his awareness of being in a false position so constantly haunted by the hollowness of all he had placed is faith in.

As Henry Popkin has pointed out, the references to nature and manual work 'forms the chief repository of Miller's positive values'. According to Popkin, though these bits of talk and action are brief and not entirely coherent. It seems that they are quite sufficiently coherent and no more fragmentary than the form of the play requires them to be. With its nightmarish shutting between present and past, the play may seem less coherent then **All My Sons**. In fact, it is less tightly but more powerfully structured and the montage is thoroughly germane to Miller's purpose. It is because of the structure and the development of situation, which it encourages, that the language is seldom disappointing as it is so often at the climax of **All My Sons.**

The one scene which demands powerful language is the last night seed planting scene, at the end of the play. Willy is aware that he has ignored for too long the call of the open air, which he pathetically tries to plant seeds by torch light. The poetry spreads from the action to the language, which is simple, unpretentious and innocent of any rhetorical inflation, but pregnant, specific, and thoroughly effective.

Unfortunately, not all the writing is on this level. Linda, the patient and loyal wife; charley, the patient and loyal neighbour, neither of them are developed to their full potential characters both have flatly rhetorical speeches in defense of Willy.

Willy Loman was a 'flamed' character in the sense he did not reconcile himself to the environment, which in its operability ran against his cherished ideas. Willy Loman found the environment greatly flawed in the sense of the lack of human response, filial disobedience and the impersonal nature of the commercial world. When he found himself failing in the business along with his sons getting alienated from him; and his body losing its youthful drive and vitality, he ends his life. Even as he did so, he continued to entertain the good of his wife and two sons by leaving behind the insurance money for them. Arthur Miller has projected **Death of a Salesman** in such a way as to show the intensity of tragic element in the personality of Willy Loman. In one way, he can be called a 'privileged' salesman who refused to be commodified and dehumanized.

Arthur Miller has a point in saying "that tragedy is the consequence of man's total compulsion to evaluate himself justly, his destruction in the attempt posits a wrong or an evil in his environment. And this is precisely the morality of tragedy and its lesson. This discovery of the moral law, which is what the enlightenment of tragedy, is not the discovery of some abstract or metaphysical quantity" (Robert a. Martin 5).

Precisely, Arthur Miller in visualizing the image of Willy Loman thought of an enormous face the height of the proscenium arch apparently implying an extra-large face of a human being carrying the burden of the weird contradictions of modern social life. Once a man is commodified or propelled by the money – value as such, his instincts get defiled, twisted and tortured by moment – to – moment meanness. Precisely, Willy Loman as the play projects is not obsessed with the greed for money. He needed money for survival for himself and his family with honour and comfortable life-continuity. But he was denied much in his advanced age which made him to opt for death; and he did so in terms of his cherished love feeling for the sake of his family members. In spite of the insulting behaviour of his two sons, he was not hard on them. It all shows that he was filled with graceful feelings for them.

If the inhospitable and erratic environment distracted Willy Loman much and then, set him on the path of self-destruction, it is equally valid to say that Miller considered bad social conditions, and perverted attitudes responsible for man's suffering and alienation in the modern world. Another facet of the crystal, which is frequently illuminated by the montage of scenes, is the relationship between sexual activity and guilt. Eric Bentley has suggested that the use of sex serves to mask the social criticism in the play and to offer an alternative explanation of the disaster that be fall the protagonist. On the contrary, that all through the play Miller uses sex as a means of carrying his social argument forward. Willy, Biff and Happy all behave badly over sexual relationships. Miller demonstrates very effectively how the bad behavior reflects their social conditioning and expresses their resentment of the role society forces them to play.

The failure of Willy's relationship with Linda is closely linked to his failure as a salesman. He believes, wrongly, that he needs to sell himself to her, to impress her by big talk. Even at the time he was doing relatively well, he was barely able to keep ahead of their hire - purchase commitments, but he always talked as though he were doing better than he really was. In spite of her love, she was never able to convince him that he was good enough for her as he actually was, in himself, and it was partly his failure to impress her as much as he felt she needed to be impressed that drove him into the arms of other women. To them he could boast without himself to them with wire cracks and gifts of silk stockings.

The illuminations of the man are so exquisitely molded into the form of the play that it sweeps along like a powerful tragic symphony. The actors are attuned to the text as if they were distinct instruments. Themes rise and fade, are varied and repeated. Again as in music, an idea may be introduced as a faint echo, and afterward developed to its fullest part in the big scheme. It is difficult to imagine anyone more splendid than Lee J. Cobb is as Willy Loman, the salesman. To be big and broken is so contradictory. The actor subtly moves from the first realization of defeat, into a state of stubborn jauntiness alternating with childlike fear in a magnificent portrait of obsolescence. Willy's wife, Linda is a truthfully blocked out character, gentle and delicate, yet fiercely loving and fiercely loyal. The scenes where she defends and explains the father to her sons are done with heart wringing reality.

The play seems to demand total commitment to success without any regard for human values. It indicts a system which will eat the orange and throw away the peel. The system is symbolized in that wears out and break down, and Willy is unable to afford a new one. Willy cherishes the car by polishing it. The road the car leads to unopened territories, not lending anywhere beside which the woods burn. Willy's dilemma is not purely social, it has psychological implications. Willy Loman gradually destroys himself with spurious beliefs conforming to the artificial standards of reality. As the name suggests, Willy Loman, stands for a low and ordinary man, because his life reveals the tragedy of every common man. Willy Loman's average and drab life, his commitment to the standard ideals, to the standard commercial products, and even to the standard language highlight his adherence to the phoney aspect of the society.

Alas S. Downer had said that Willy has ever imperfectly known himself. He is a little man not cut out for big issues of life. He has chosen the wrong goal and the irony is that despite the consciousness of the direction, he moves in. He pursues the dream with all intensity of passion which, in the process, destroys his vision. The road and Willy's car, for all the social and psychological significance, have metaphysical meaning. Willy's soul can no longer travel because the road has lost meaning. Willy's commitment to his values is total. Willy realizes his own hollowness and yet his commitment is so absolute that he is perhaps incapable of turning his whole life and admitting his failure. He comes to realize that the value of fatherhood can be best realized by giving up his life by money for his son. Lois Gordon has appropriately commented that

Death of a salesman is a drama of a man's journey into himself; it is a man's emotional recapitulation of the experiences that have shaped him and his values, a man's confession of the dreams to which he has been committed; and it is also a man's attempt to confront, in what is ultimately a metaphysical sense, the meaning of his life and the nature of his universe (Lois Gordon 280).

It is worth quoting Arthur Miller's explanation of how Willy is driven to his death by this revelation of love

In this he is given his existence, so to speak, his father hood, for which he has always striven and which until now he could not achieve. That, he is unable to talk victory thoroughly to his heart, that it closes the circle for him and propels him to his death, it is the wage of his sin, which was to have committed himself so completely to the counterfeits of dignity and the false coinage emotional in his idea of success that he can prove his existence only by best owning 'power' on his posterity, a power deriving from the sale of his last asset, himself for the price of his insurance policy (65).

The end of the play satisfies thoughts which are ironical. Willy dies to gain insurance money. He sells himself. His death in this sense is ironical. But it is also an act of supreme sacrifice and of the assertion of man's identity and dignity in a selfish and malignant social system. Altogether the selling in the play proves to be a much more useful dramatic currency than the 'pipe – dreams' in Eugene O' Neill's. **The Iceman Cometh**, to which it is roughly comparable. But in the selling, the words are always for more closely welded to action.

CHAPTER FOUR

CONCLUSION

Arthur Miller's main object in writing the play **Death of a Salesman** is to portray in all nakedness the American society with all its successes and failures that causes tragedy for the people like Willy Loman. It would be more appropriate to call it a play representing the failure myth than success myth.

Arthur Miller, however, took a different stance from what writers like Horatio Alger did to glorify the success myth in their novels. Miller had experienced the ravages of the great depression of the1930's and so his adverse reaction against the success myth is clearly expounded in **Death of a Salesman**. Miller personifies in uncle Ben the American dream of success. As Ben puts it to prove this success myth.

Ben : William, when I walked into the jungle I was seventeen.

When I walked out I was twenty one, and by God I was rich (31).

Miller himself has said "Willy Loman is I think a person who embodies in him some of the most terrible conflicts running through the streets of American today"(72). Harbod Clurman also echoes this view. The technique adopted by Arthur Miller in this play is a little bit complicated. Robert Hogan pays a high tribute to the technical excellence of the play.

Arthur Miller also discusses the concept of 'the tragic victory'. He repudiates the idea that a man who sacrifices himself for a cause should make the audience feel some kind of elevation. Man's death is terrifying thing and should not bring joy to anyone. But, he says, in a great variety of ways even death, the ultimate negative, can be an assertion of bravery. Willy according to Miller has achieved a very powerful piece of knowledge, which is that he is loved by his son, and has been embraced by him and forgiven. In this he is given his existence, so to speak, his father hood, for which he has always striven and which until now he could not achieve. The standards of magnificence and truth have gone through a change in modern age. Miller, indeed, is sensitive modern, and meant his play to be a tragedy. But his conception at tragedy is different.

According to Beirman, Hart and Johnson "unlike the dramas by Sophocles, Shakespeare, and Lorca, Arthur Miller's **Death of a Salesman** is a tragedy set in our times, played out on our own scene, by characters who, however, we regard that quality of their thought, speak in our own languages and with our own peculiar accents"(45). All the three consider this play a Modern Tragedy which suits modern age.

Prof. George de Schweinting regards the play as both tragedy and epic. He says, "The World" or "Universe" of **Death of a Salesman**... shows as basically traditional and epic and tragic structure in that its poles or value are clearly located and distinguished one from another in that they are also clearly objectified as in the older tradition, but not allegorized, since realistic drama stops short of tolerating allegory, and finally in that these poles of values so located and objectified, precipate the tragic situation and given a sense of "Universe" in the theories of unresolved and agony" (The New York World Telegram. P 16 Feb. 11, 1949).

William Hawkins says "**Death of a Salesman** is a play written along the lines of the finest classical tragedy. It is the revelation of man's downfall, in destruction whose roots are entirely in his own resolution for this man in this life. The play is fervent query into the great competitive dream of success, as it strips to the core a castaway from the race for recognition and money". (The New York World Magazine P. 16 Feb. 11, 1949).

Miller's departure from the Athenian Tragedy is seen in his emphasis on the moral law that shapes human conditions and destroys men. His comment on the nature of tragic flaw conforms to his idea of modern tragedy. The common man, Miller is of the view that it is not a subject below the treatment of tragedy. But what is essential is that the tragic action should stem from the fact that the hero is inherently unwilling to remain passive. Like most modern tragedians, Miller seeks a new explanation of the human situation with its tragic aspects in naturalistic and humanistic terms, not transcendental ones. He has been giving his common man tragic status and the result has been a strengthening and an intensifying of the tragic quality in his plays.

The main objective of Miller is to discard surface realism to achieve theatrical expression and to establish deeper realities. **Death of a Salesman** is a play of dreams in which the use of the expressionist technique is essential. The hallucination bringing back to Willy's mind his past is highly expressionist in content.

Psychoanalytically, the technique adopted is to highlight the disintegration of human personality. The flashbacks complete the perfection of technique. According to Raymond Williams, the technique adopted is a blend of expressionism and realism. This play concerning the degeneration of a family is about the highly sophisticated American life.

The stability of a family depends on the type of life led by the father. For good or evil, it should set a pattern in the house; otherwise one cannot see anything else except the broken homes. This is a remarkable thing set forth by Arthur Miller in **Death of a Salesman.**

According to Schneider, Miller has tried to project in this play the guilt of a younger brother for his hared; this would mean Willy's constant comparison of Biff's progress with Charley's son.

Willy Loman is a queer combination of Marlowe's Faustus. Because, Faustus sells his soul to Lucifer for the purpose of gaining necromantic knowledge. Like Faustus, here Loman sells his soul for the purpose of gaining insurance money. He is an anti - romantic hero involved in an action that takes place in a romantic setting. The character of the protagonist is slowly and steadily laid bare to the eye and mind of the reader.

In this play, Willy Loman stands as the monument of a frustrated individual under the stress of modern civilization. Linda, his wife, calls attention to this fact in the Requiem scene. She calls her husband a good man. They are now free, the house being paid for. Biff too realizes the goodness of his father and says that Willy "had the wrong dreams all, all, wrong"(104). What Miller attempts to portray through the play is to expose American capitalism. Play is an 'anatomy of failure' and a 'elegy' on the successes. The unavoidable tragic note is clearly shown in **Death of a Salesman**.

It shows man as a victim of a commercial society, who fall as a prey to capitalistic ideals. The aging Loman, the protagonist of the play, meets with his tragic end because he is baffled by a life time of failure in a society which values only success. To some critics, Loman represents the failure of the American Dream, but most others he represents the ambitious but in practical mass of people who allow themselves to be destroyed by a corrupt and evil society. The main reason for Loman's tragedy is the placing of his trust in false values that must flop one day or the other.

There is a universal significance in Loman's situation. He has lived passionately for values, but soon discovers that they are false. He comes to realize the absurdity of human life and variety of all human endeavours. Having gained the knowledge that men like him cannot survive in such a society, he attempts to save his personal dignity by selling his most previous ware, that is himself. Willy Loman represents everyman living in a materialistic society, who has to wage a battle against the odds in life to make his life purposeful and meaningful.

A tragedy serves as an eye - opener to others. After Willy's suicide, Biff ceases to daydream. At the graveyard, he determines to give up his irresponsible ways and discipline himself and work hard. He decides to live away from home so that he will not be a burden to his aged mother. As for Happy, he too swears that he will work hard and reach his father's ideal of being the number one man. Charley who used to be very caustic towards Willy forgives him now, saying that dreaming is not only part of a salesman's profession but the very essence of the American psyche. Charley thus gives up his vitriol comments and becomes kind of Willy. The changes in others that Willy could not bring about during his life are effected by his death. Thus Miller through Willy at the end proves as an eye opener not only to his family and neighbours but also to the audience and makes **Death of a Salesman** a Modern tragedy.

BIBLIOGRAPHY

PRIMARY SOURCE

Miller, Arthur. Death of a Salesman. New Delhi : UBSPD, 2003.

SECONDARY SOURCES

Arthur, K. Oberg. American Expressionistic Drama. Delhi : Doba House, 1970.

Brater, Enoch. Arthur Miller; A Playwright's Life and Works. Newyork : Thames and Hudson, 2005.

Brustein, Robert. American Expressionistic Drama. Delhi : Doba House, 1970.

Dr. Dutta, Usha . Arthur Miller, As a Critic of Drama. New Delhi: Ammol Publication Pvt. Ltd, 2000.

Gassner, John. Tragedy in the Modern Theatre. New York: Crown Publishers, 1954.

Gordon, Lois. Death of a Salesman: An Appreciation. Florida: Everest/ Edwards. Inc, 1969.

Gottfried, Martin. Arthur Miller: His Life and Work. Cambridge: MA: Da Capo Press, 2003.

Gould, Jean. Modern American Ploywrights. Bombay: Ubsons Printers, 1969.

Griffin, Alice. Understanding Arthur Miller. Columbia: University of South Carolina Press, 1996 .

Hayman, Ronald. Arthur Miller. London : Heinemamn Educational Books Limited, 1970.

Hogan, Robert. Arthur Miller. Minneapolis: University of Minnesto Press, 1964.

Koon, Helane. Twentieth Century Interpretations of Death of a Salesman: A Collection of Critical Essays. Englewood Cliffs: Prentice – Hall, 1983.

Koorey, Stefani. Arthur Millers Life and Literature: An Annotated and Comprehensive Guide. Lanham, Md: Scarecrow Press, 2000.

Krieger, Murray. The Tragic Vision: The Confrontation of Extremity. Batimore: The John Hopkins University Press, 1973.

Krutch, Joseph Wood. The Modern Temper A Study and A Confession. New York: Harcourt, Brace and Company, 1956.

Longely John Lewis, The Tragic Mask: A Study of Faulkner's Heroes. Chapel Hill: The University of North Carolina Press, 1963.

Martin, A. Robert., and R. Steven Centela. The Theatre Essays of Arthur Miller. New York: De Copo Press, 1996.

Martine, J. James. Critical Essays on Arthur Miller. Boston: G.K. Hall & Co, 1979.

Miller, Arthur. The Theatre Essays of Arthur Miller. New York: Viking Press, 1978.

Mottram, Eric. American Expressionistic Drama. Delhi : Doaba House, 1970.

Murray, Edward. Arthur Miller dramatist. New York: F. Ungar Pub. Co, 1967.

Pandey, K. Mithilesh. Studies in Contemporary Literature. New Delhi: Ammol Publications, 2002.

Roudane C. Matthew. Conversations with Arthur Miller. USA: University Press of Mississppi Jackson and London, 1987.

Secker and Warburg. Arthur Miller: Collected Plays. London: The Cresset Press, 1967.

Wilson, Edwin. The Theatre Experience. New York: McGraw Hill Book Company, 1980.

Wimsatt, K. William., and Cleanth Brookes. Literary Criticism : A Short History. London: Oxford Book Company, 1957.

Journals

Jackson, Esther Merle. Death of a Salesman: Tragic Myth. C.L.A Journal 7, No.1. Sep 1963.

Miller, Arthur. Tragedy and Common Man. The New York Times. Feb 27, 1949, II.

Popkin, Henry. Arthur Miller : The Strange Encounter. The Sewance Review, Winter 1960.

9 798885 693981

Printed by Libri Plureos GmbH in Hamburg, Germany